MIRACLE MOMENTS IN
BASKETBALL

KENNY ABDO

Fly!
An Imprint of Abdo Zoom
abdobooks.com

abdobooks.com

Published by Abdo Zoom, a division of ABDO, P.O. Box 398166, Minneapolis, Minnesota 55439. Copyright © 2022 by Abdo Consulting Group, Inc. International copyrights reserved in all countries. No part of this book may be reproduced in any form without written permission from the publisher. Fly!™ is a trademark and logo of Abdo Zoom.

Printed in the United States of America, North Mankato, Minnesota.
052021
092021

THIS BOOK CONTAINS RECYCLED MATERIALS

Photo Credits: Alamy, AP Images, Getty Images, Icon Sportswire, iStock, Newscom, Shutterstock
Production Contributors: Kenny Abdo, Jennie Forsberg, Grace Hansen
Design Contributors: Dorothy Toth, Neil Klinepier

Library of Congress Control Number: 2020919626

Publisher's Cataloging-in-Publication Data

Names: Abdo, Kenny, author.
Title: Miracle moments in basketball / by Kenny Abdo
Description: Minneapolis, Minnesota : Abdo Zoom, 2022 | Series: Miracles in sports | Includes online resources and index.
Identifiers: ISBN 9781098223199 (lib. bdg.) | ISBN 9781098223892 (ebook) | ISBN 9781098224240 (Read-to-Me ebook)
Subjects: LCSH: Basketball--History--Juvenile literature. | Basketball--Records-Juvenile literature. | Sports--History--Juvenile literature. | Miracles--Juvenile literature. | Curiosities and wonders--Juvenile literature.
Classification: DDC 796.323--dc23

TABLE OF CONENTS

BASKETBALL

From driveways to packed arenas, basketball boxes out all other sports!

On a rainy day in 1891, Canadian gym teacher James Naismith looked for a way to keep his class busy. He found a peach basket and had the students toss a ball into it for points.

Buzzer beaters and untouchable records are some of the miracles that have changed basketball forever.

DO YOU BELIEVE?

Magic Johnson was 20 years old during game 6 of the 1980 **Finals**. He scored 42 points, had seven assists, and handled 15 rebounds. That was unheard of for a **rookie**. Johnson led the Lakers to win the NBA **title** that year.

NATIONAL BASKETBALL
ASSOCIATION

AND

SPORT MAGAZINE'S
MOST VALUABLE PLAYER AWARD

1980
WORLD CHAMPIONSHIP
SERIES

EARVIN "MAGIC" JOHNSON

In 1986, Ralph Sampson hit one of the luckiest shots in NBA history. With a tied score and one second left on the clock, Sampson caught the ball and hit the **layup**, winning the game for the Rockets.

Michael Jordan finished his Bulls career strongly with the final shot he made for the team. Down by one point, Jordan made a deciding shot over Bryon Russell with just seven seconds to go. They won, making it Jordan's sixth and last **Finals** victory.

In 2009, Kobe Bryant hit a miracle **buzzer beater** from behind the arc. The incredible shot won the game for the Lakers, beating the Heat by a close 108–107.

The Cavaliers were down 3-1 in the series against the Warriors in the 2016 NBA **Finals**. The Cavs took the next three games to win the series, making them the only team to overcome that large of a **deficit** in Finals history.

LEGACY

Most basketball miracles are preserved in books and highlight reels. ESPN's *30 for 30* series focused on NC State coach Jim Valvano's winning nine **do-or-die** games in a row. Seven of which the team was losing in the final minute.

Basketball has come a long way from
peach baskets. But what hasn't changed
is the possibility of witnessing miracles
on the court.

GLOSSARY

buzzer beater – a shot scored at the very last second of a basketball quarter.

deficit – the amount of points that a team is losing by.

do-or-die – when the only two options are success or failure.

Finals – the championship series of the NBA where the team who wins best-of-seven games is determined champions of the year.

layup – a onehanded shot made from right under the basket.

rookie – an athlete during their first full season of their sport.

title – a first-place position in a contest.

ONLINE RESOURCES

Booklinks
NONFICTION NETWORK
FREE! ONLINE NONFICTION RESOURCES

To learn more about miracle moments in basketball, please visit abdobooklinks.com or scan this QR code. These links are routinely monitored and updated to provide the most current information available.

INDEX